Postcards and

emails

Postcards and emails

Poems by
Nick Sparrow

Published by

Pewter Rose Press

www.pewter-rose-press.com

First published in Great Britain 2013

Collection © Nick Sparrow

ISBN 9781908136404

Printed and bound in Great Britain

Front cover artwork of Nottingham Council House © Kat Sparrow

Dedicated to my daughters Katherine and Rebecca

Early inspiration from Rebecca Sparrow:
'To Daddy I hope you like this flower I have made for you I think you will like it. Lot of love from Rebecca'

Acknowledgements

I thank Nick Hedderly, Ruth Fainlight and Dee Reynolds for their kind comments on my work and Anne McDonnell at Pewter Rose Press for helping with the publication. Any faults in the text are my own.

Introduction

The poems in this chapbook collection, being a gift to my friends, range from my first poem written in 2002 to my prize winning Time in 2012. The poems were all born in the pockets of my old travelling bag rather than an ivory tower. I would follow John Clare more than DH Lawrence, and am glad to be an occasional pedlar of poems.

Several have been previously published in Lowdham Writers' Group anthologies, of which group I am currently chair. One was included in a Southwell Poetry & Prose Evening booklet with proceeds to Oxfam. One was generously read on BBC Radio Nottingham by my friend Sue Laver. Many have been read by me at poetry events around Nottinghamshire. These are the latest versions.

Back in 2005 I won the Nottingham Literary Consultancy Free Read Scheme prize for my novel The Beach Party and I would really like to be a novelist! The reviewer said 'I was sorry to finish – and want to know how it ends.' I still intend to finish that novel.

Contents

Nottingham

Life and times

In Spain and Portugal

A romance of Aljezur

A mirror for Portugal

Poets and places

Return to Shell Island

Return to Shell Island
and catch a whisper
of young days
when Nature's soft
benevolent brush
first painted
an outline for my life,
since dedicated, I have found,
to loving her.

Look to Harlech
and the distant necklace of Lleyn
whose hills are rubbed out
as storms blow in
from the Atlantic,
and white waves roll to shore
in a paradise of colour,
as the sun comes out again
to light the hills of Mawddach.

Respect Idris,
the bad tempered giant
glowering in his mountain fortress
to catch trippers unawares
with a blast of rain at Barmouth,
while the coastal train
rumbles over the estuary trestle
and racing tides invade
Idris's flowery garden.

In sing song Welsh
the tollbooth lady promises
fine wea-ther, soon,
for the trestle crossing
to Fairbourne,
where the sun already glitters
on sandbanks of apricot hue,
and shallows turn green
blue from Abermawr.

Now to be alive!
In infant school
I was always gazing
out of windows, they said,
unspoilt by progress then
I was making plans
for summer shell collecting
and my own lessons,
with ten shells out of ten.

From the bridge at Clappergate

Here leaps the arch of stone,
so lean on the parapet
where waters fall jolly,
thrilled to fill
soundings
in kettles below.

In the eye of the river
swim, swim,
bow to its fiddle,
shoals for laughter
as light
splashes in.

Little fish, listen,
jump the
cold heart where
languid upwellings
pump fear
of deep dark.

Time glitters and
turns to stone,
only bubbles
can stay
as reason
flows away.

So swim,
jack to river's queen,
joy ripples
unseen as water
falls anyway
at Clappergate.

For St Michael's, Stretton-en-le-field

Your sunny graveyard
is a grassed meadow,
and stones are warmed
remembering happy times,
when elmy shades
brought Sunday people
to sing with flowers,
and a chap
from down the lane
came to mow
the grass again.

Now stand on tiptoe,
and peep in at the window
by the padlocked door,
where a queer light
plays unobserved
on a tracery of arches,
that feign surprise
at dust gathered lately
on pale box pews,
as stalls of a barn
wait for a harvest.

Yet the lectern still carries
the Bible open at a page,
and a spider shivers hollow
in the casement,
grown thin since April's fly,
when a fat agricultural treat
last came by,
now, cobwebby and dry.
How long, she asks,
until July, when some new fly
might come in and die?

Once such webs
were brushed away.
Now the community
of patient
churchyard souls
petitions me,
single representative
of the living,
to go for a key
that opens the door,
to let people in again.

There's hope
I read in a notice
to the folk gathered here,
of a service in September,
when the minister
is coming
to open the lock
the blacksmith made,
so the living can
sing in tune again
with the dead.

Meanwhile,
June has sent
all her swallows
to tumble by the steeple,
and bees go lazy
at the gate.
Drowse on, summer,
and make
us grateful,
send a fly
for the spider who waits.

Exeter Arms, Derby

Fill and empty
this glass of experience
bless the Exeter Arms
sole saving
watering hole on a
quiet startled street
cut off at the ring road
and paradise for
beer and thirst
to meet.

New gods
save these hanging baskets
and deliver me capable yet
to sun dimmed interiors
where swirls of
golden barley
are meadows
fermented into pools
and easy are the voices
at bar tops and stools.

Write only
what we know,
of pubs, women and fags.
I gave up once but
I'll have one Ruth,
there's no danger in that.
Your dark eyes
would know me longer
but where can I
lay my hat?

Your boyfriend
is at the fruit machine,
a lemon not to
care for you enough.
Have a tonic, Ruth,
we're fifty
and can sigh for pubs
that will never be,
and other lives and loves,
that want us home for tea.

I love you deeply
Exeter Arms,
new gods set us free,
for endless afternoons
of pleasure,
for Ruth,
her boyfriend,
my wife,
these flowering baskets
and me.

Norfolk Poems

Overstrand, Norfolk

Standing by his pots,
the fisherman said
lobsters are up the lane me beauty,
not here. At the shop, you can't miss it.
Behind him the pearl green sea
rolled on off the cliffs,
driven by an east wind.

At the slipway

The squealing is a school party
playing along on the beach.
At the slipway, a rusted tractor
attends with trailer and fishing boat.
No moving part can escape the salt
you'd think, but deep inside,
steel and oil will turn today.

On the Common

Grassy West Runton Common
waits before rain
as a flint built cottage looks on.
A blackbird
having eaten his fill of fruit
shakes his feathers in a briar,
then flies to complain.

Wheelers Bay

Evening and absolutely still,
except for cicadas like spoked
bicycle wheels going round at night,
and waves making love on the beach,
slowly rolling in, rolling out
pebbles in the undertow,
all still except

for dissolving light
at sea horizon,
where day's end is night beginning
and steeped cloud is orange,
waiting for the first star, her lover,
absolutely still
except

for lights ashore in twos and threes,
from holiday house verandas
and a fisherman's cot,
closed up now,
then wow! The brave lighthouse,
sends a beam at huge darkness
but night has no champion,

only a navigation light at jetty end,
looking with red eye to sea
for boats,
or just lobster pot buoys,
their catch waving claws
until morning,
all quiet except

for the luminous moon rising,
car headlight up the lane
soft engine labouring,
every shadowed bank
broadcasting a cicada's
thirst for oil
on ratchet, gear and cog,

otherwise
silent up the lane,
last sea sound fading
from the cliff,
any face a blur,
hotel
just around the corner.

Summer Hill

Now ends the longest day
and in quiet woods
a black feather fallen
on sunlit trails
is summer mystery.

Black, crow black
and sun gold sun,
paint the track
and myriad leaves
just one summer old.

On hill top,
feather skies are turquoise,
dreams harvest a wheat field,
and a solitary crow and I
keep the day's cause yet.

Yes, quick breeze lifts to
cool the parching dust,
colours flare like refineries
and swifts empty air
for bed.

Night climbs summer hill,
no one stays too long
and later on,
car headlights will
probe the winking suburb.

Rose

The wild rose flowers again.

We know how love comes
crashing through the brake
but stops here,
these blooms just advertise
rose petal cheeks for kissing.

At your root
where lovers
are often buried,
words make compost
for your glory.

Accept these words
in due token then,
just a petal,
a flower,
a thought.

In the Great Oak

Up the year crowned hill
there's a miracle in the
compass of branches.
In your bough swept circle,
whose sense approaches?

Deep rooted,
the oracle receives me
wood to wood
bole on bole
as life with life connects,
its vital voice
speaks to me,
what was, what is,
what next?

Now is the season
it says
for small loves.
Small loves are grained the deepest.
No rains stop the acorn of desire
as in the rhyming branches,
the whispers
are my own.

In Autumn

An autumn afternoon
and a butterfly
takes nectar
from a dahlia,
knowing an
enduring power
that works in the
body of a flower,
and in the strength
of beating wings,
returning colour
unasked for
like a kiss.

Came a frost
last night yet
red on red
spills the dahlia,
all petals
opportune
and willing,
to keep a promise
in marriage
with the sun,
where once joined,
no kisses are
undone.

Everywhere Brighton

On the high speed train
reading Satanic Verses
every station feels like Brighton
stopping to start again.

Sunlight flashes through trees
burning hot on wheat fields
and river lakes
breeze rippled and reed bent.

On we go, your lake is my window,
love levels the landscape
and fills all the woods
with desire.

Hickling Village

Mark the twittering swallows,
young birds, September's brood,
gathering from rooftops
along the telegraph wires,
their backs to the whistling starlings,
who'll stay when
skies turn cumulonimbus
and last flights down main street
stir thoughts of Africa.
Look up, and they are already gone.

Dickens' house and the jay

That green door, rather severe,
to forty eight Doughty Street
where a tree quietly
sprouts a leafy
spreading canopy in the
warm London sun.

From that happy, bijou forest
a jay hops
branch to branch,
balustrade to balcony,
fixing with bright eye
any opportunity

For acorns
in window boxes.
So city smart,
fashionable,
in blue cap and wings
he strides up and down

peering in at panes
to shuttered rooms
where chandeliers
or candlesticks
arouse intense avian
curiosity.

A quill reflects awry
in mirrored glass,
he pulls and cleans it,
preening to perfection
a streetwise plumage
already inky neat.

The jay turns a page or two,
though the house
is shut for dust.
Is he Dickens's jay
returning, to haunt
the window box and panes?

And was it written,
that our spirits will revisit
the arcades and places
we went
in the leafy noontime
of our days?

For John Clare

A wandering lane for your thoughts,
through stubble and ploughed land
labouring dawn to dusk
with woods a smoking blue,
August silver gold
and trees a pool of shade.

Poetry was here,
now my train
scythes a straight line from
Grantham to Peterborough,
flashing by Helpston Halt
and your lost river.

Gods and goddesses

In Cheshire

Away from chaos
the land is woven
with stories,
fold on fold,
broken with gold,
where black cattle move slowly
down to shade to drink,
and stand to
contemplate milking.

These skies have strode
manfully from
far contentious hills.
Be with me Minerva,
just touch, as
a river carries itself
to the sea and
water finds water
in brilliant combination.

On a Dee's reach
at swans landing,
between old bridge
and new,
rushes quiver
to stillness
as flood waters
scythe
through.

Here a sanctuary then.
If I sleep at
your shrine
on a grassy mound shaded,
Goddess
press a thought
on mine,
of arts divine,
and swans.

Mars and Earth

I am Mars the terrible,
red planet and god of war,
see my dust, beautiful
in your southern skies,
when Earth's night
is my tender sunrise.

Lately, barren sister,
you have grown life
and our heavens dance
is not the same,
your moonlit perfection
is stained with blue.

As we move apart
I have just one doubt.
Is there an ocean
or an air
that blows,
to make my dust live?

Brother Mars,
I was always pregnant
with minerals
and when I gave birth
to life my children
all came wriggling out.

Now I am round
with life and
birds thrill to
sing in my treetops,
so no nights here
are ever silent.

My airy ocean
is of the heart,
where the Mars of war
would shroud it.
Still I carry lust
for you, in my streets.

The muse

She comes like a flame
to a moth.

See two choices before me,
to ask forgiveness for sin,
or meet her promise and carry me off,
as night illuminates passion.

Dark ending, how I need extinction,
occasioned some bookish afternoon,
when she turns a page and finds me,
flying out, round the room.

She knows, she knows
she has me,
contained for leisured research,
held willingly, so that

from her dressing table,
should evening flame entice,
she'll lift my lid and take me,
to moth flame paradise.

Nottingham

Symphony in grey

Part I

Parliament Street
blares a dissonant horn
at late crossed pedestrians
and a five o'clock fog
that lifts to roof height
with melancholy and the
squeal of bus brakes.

My beautiful queue
dissolves in departures,
where only I recall
lunchtime and the
New Castle carillon
tuning up with a
bing-bong bing-bong
for a single bell at one,
answered by
far notes from
the London train,
leaving us
with a bye-bye!

Oh, the dazzle of lights
through so many fractions
of lives.
When will celebrity art
in the gallery
have more to say than this?
Parliament Street at bus time,
waiting,
grey bliss.

Part II

Broadmarsh
daytime shoppers' metropolis
rises bleak, bright
and naked as ashes,
to turn its back on me,
a toil shouldered Caliban.

Echoes sound at night,
its empty cloak
and acetylene lights
are filled with
timeless arrogance,
slabs for pagan sacrifice.

But when blazing sun fires
bring temptation to glow,
Lowry mauve skies
scatter pigeon's wings
across those flat heads.

Walk, and
silk breezes blow,
when we come to
breathe the night stars,
Broadmarsh can be
lovely in our sight.

Let there be nothing to fear.
Only these arts
make it beautiful
and reconcile
this living with
the night.

Part III

My travelling companion
the Midland Railway station
slips past the bus
tiled soft burnt pink,
as a dinky skirted girl
catches the heart's
transport link.

Suns wreck and sink
in distant oceans,
cloud islands
drift blood orange and
puffs of smoke leak
from steamboats to China.
Thin rain streams
past my window,
each drop a prism
running an
underwater
silent film.

On Trent Bridge
streetlights reflect
oil the colour of cormorants,
who dive for fish
in welters of water
to the river bed,
vanishing
beneath the constant moon.

I lost my place in a book
and will forget my umbrella.
But in this symphony of grey,
where I spent the day,
the only answer
to my question is,
keep a warm heart.

Blackberry in winter

A town is a smaller place in winter,
back yards to a twitchel
keep their secrets bolted
and bicycles are chained in sheds
or pedalled, bent to a devilish sky.

At the riverside my once fruitful cousins
shrink from floods and
bare a thorny waste at footballers
who cry 'Man on! Man on!'
then stumble defeated into cars.

As the old black tower on the hill
grows dim and swept with rain
a seagull signals end of day
with memories of waves and rocking boats.
But I am grateful in my twitchel thicket,

for deep dry mould and fragrant rotted leaves
where quickened shoots
and last year's briars are a fortress
of dreams and bloody mindedness,
in dark battle with all the sleets of winter.

And I know that in cellars, gallons of wine
await cork squeaking release
and jams offer sweet seductive pleasure
to toasted crumpets
in a hundred overheated WI halls.

Bed, preserve of the wicked,
is a warm furrow on late mornings
and early nights when only
sin drives the leaping candle
and stars gleam from ceilings all night.

Know that the blackberry will come again
before you know it, even now
ready for the punk, raven haired,
berry lipped fairy,
whose wish turns winter to wine.

Winter fruit

A weak December dawn,
and the only tree in the square
straggles six leaves to the wind
and a clutch of apricot balloons,
that escaped a party late maybe
and lost their way home.

Like perfect grapes
I thought, strange winter fruit
blown like myself
in transit.

January memorial

Springy is the turf
in the cemetery,
viridian with stone
sharps and flats,

waxen gleams the ivy
at the monument,
rhyming a melody
in silence to the facts,

of a railway
superintendent
and his family,
happily now departed all,

who rest in
moss-velvet solitude,
with squirrels finding
acorns, that fall.

The big freeze

Winter gathers about the town in snow.
At midday down frozen paths
slanting sun warms the snow capped
top of a Bulwell stone wall,
at eye level
dripping to reveal mossy crags,
and tiny velvet worlds of gleaming green
wilderness under splinters of ice,
it's a tundra,
where polar bears might stop and stare,
scenting my own hibernation
and knowing that
tonight, it will freeze again.

November Cotswold hills

November morning's bus stop,
and risen with the moon
still gleaming on
last red apples and
boughs, with leaves stripped
and night lost in gardens,
as up comes the number six.

At Trent Bridge island
seagulls flap for
takeaways in the
surge of lorries and cars,
that ebb and flow
around the pedestrian refuge,
as waves roll by in dreams.

You fat geese warm up and
parade the muddy promenade.
Me, I remember
with sudden affection
the weekend now gone by
and its wintery, leaf strewn
Cotswold hills.

Kaleidoscope

In the arboretum
the water sprinkler throws rainbows,
pop, pop, pop
at baking beds and lawns,
wetting the asphalt
and making shrubs drip
to the gardener's tune.

Skirting the leaping spray
and jumping these
red-hot pokers,
the evergreen oak
draws me to its deep shade
and slopes sown all over with
bottle tops, fag ends and ring pulls.

Sleep comes drowsing
Under a kaleidoscopic
canopy of leaves,
while footballers kick about
and distant voices
remind us that
lunchtimes are ever short.

Woken suddenly,
brazen in the afternoon
two teenage prostitutes
come to blag a cigarette
or just one pound eighty,
with their knowing and unlikely tale
of a friend who let them down.

Unhelpfully,
I truly have no money
and don't even smoke.
Come on! says one
to the other with scorn,
let's get back to the street,
and she falls off her high heel.

The shop mannequin

Take the stone flag passage
past three granite columns
with flowered capitals,
to a narrow arcade,

where through plate glass
a mannequin with attitude
models a little black dress
and pearl necklace,

one hand placed
provocatively on hip,
all of it for sale,
to dare you go in?

Oh, I wish,
but never could I ask her out.

Life and times

A life

Let life be
rich in small things,
in days spent uncounted,
in plentiful needs and wants
in companionship of friends
in travels here and there
in gardens and flowers
in treasures for rainy days
in the passions of a lover
and bonds unbreakable
in unlikely paragons of significance
that say how to love and why to love
filling a book or music score
to reflect a life well
if ever the need to tell
of a lake, found
in a nutshell.

The lion

He was ruler of the toyshop cabinet,
king of the glass shelf,
where rows of jungle beasts
paraded with farm animals,
milkmaids and soldiers.

Oh how he roared,
ivory teeth in a snarl
curled of lip,
mane painted black and
body desert tan,
with plate sized paws
that sheathed cruel claws,
flexed, lethal and ready.

His quality was peerless,
loyal and proud
with sheer animal presence
at eye level
he forced desire to purchase.

Then roaming the carpet,
hunting gazelle by the sofa mountain
and lamp stand lake,
he was terror of the farmyard
and soldier camp,
no duster or vacuum cleaner
ever caught him.

Then one day in the wild
where children play with their mothers
in the streams and grass,
he stalked the plain
with a young hunter
who got so excited
he forgot he'd left him there.

Teatime came and went,
to find him hunting alone
in the field corner,
growl in his throat
and long tail swishing,
fierce and undaunted.

Owls hooted at night.
Centipedes reverse marched
at the lion's plastic breath and
beetles signalled from holes
or rattled off to hide.
By day, birds mistrusted
his stiff, uncompromising anger
and sang a warning.

Down all the summers
reeds burned silver on the marsh.
The farmer came to break the earth
and ploughed and ploughed again
with polished steel and winter rain,
bitten by frost
his mane turned autumn rust
and coat muddy clay.

Stiff, scary cabbages
were ranks of uniformed soldiers
who conquered the hillside
in slow manoeuvre,
vegetarians all,
the lion grunted
in pain for meat.

Until times later,
an explorer
grown older and poetic now,
came idling down the hedgerow.
Out leapt the lion to surprise him!
Ah harrrr!
They circled, wary of the gulf
grown up between them.

Can a man and lion be friends?
Can friendship be real?
Both had stories to tell!
Linnets rose twittering from the marsh
as I popped him
safely in my pocket.

Now we have Africa,
royal on a windowsill in Nottingham.

The fountain

At the ornamental lake
as sparrows wait
with the first camellias,

the fountain
worries not
for her inspiration.

Tripping the water
surface,
her life is endless.

Poetry

When the poetry rhymes to a stop,
and the customary place is empty,
when touch on touch is stilled
and only days bring arrival,
when end precedes beginning
and all we wrote is history,

then remember significance,
feel that velvet quality,
and linger
in the joy of it.

The photographer's helper

The spoiled plate,
a tarnished glass
imprisons her,
as in half a page
torn from a novel
its volume long gone missing
and forgotten.

Now fixed forever
at her workbench,
she would have had
red ribbons in her hair
and warm blood
in her finger tips,
the photographer's best helper.

The ticking clock and
ever change of calendars
kept her every evening,
waiting for his
slow patient alchemy
or some soft light to expose
her face to gaze.

But her prints never came,
spoiled by his thumb marks
and spilled spirit crystals,
he left her image on a shelf
to gather dust
put on one side
for eternity.

How cruel was that!
She never wanted
to stay a ghost
while the very last
horse drawn omnibuses
left the square for
Sneinton, or the Park.

Though it is just a photograph.
In reality she left him
that last winter afternoon
and stepped out gladly
to meet her friend
in the square
and disappear, into life.

Freedom

There is a door
leading to a garden
through a little used gate,
to the lake of enchanted bluebells.

There the nightingale
flicks his tail
clear eyed and quick,
and spills a torrent of song
from his deep summer throat.

Every leaf is freedom,
pluck one.

On opening a bottle of 1967 Russian Imperial Stout

Where have you been all my life,
resting in quiet cellars
hidden from the light and
condemnation of years?

Now here you are, upended
when all your pubs are closed
and streets empty of
mini skirts and kipper ties.

Indeed it's time gentlemen please,
to take an opener and glass
and release the exact measure of days
in a soft hiss that says

I drink, therefore I am,
Russian Imperial Stout
no less, with your nose of
Cossack boots and distant tundra flowers.

Silk oil, alcohol and licorice
are one, combined like sex
from top to bottom,
too soon gone, but not forgotten.

Time

Time, I tried to catch you
last week, but you're slippery,
and seen everywhere
in oceans
or parcelled out in parking meters,
everyone has you
in small amounts like money,
counted or given away
or stolen something rotten.

'Get up or you'll be late'
my mother often cried,
when shifting sands lasted forever
and days were imprisoned
in weeks like grains in rock,
clockface tin facists
told lies with sleight of hand,
and even the speaking clock spoke untrue,
time depended on point of view.

Once, I captured Time
in a raindrop hanging on a leaf,
he was smiling upside down
in a prism of light
along with time of day and time of life,
I said, 'You bastard Time,
how could you be so cruel to my mother?'
but he disappeared
with the approaching night.

Time, I forgive you just this once,
for time and love are the same
when chained together,
and the hour forgets,

wait, I'm almost done

You other poets

How the wandering muse brings
vast employment
of word and deed,
curried into favour
with new distillations
of sensory exotica.

Like my own small street
or garden, changed
of its loved familiar places,
what new thoughts are these,
what sorcery and magnificence,
what devilment?

Of course so many
of your poems are greater
than my own tender weeds,
my blown seeds,
trodden in pursuit
of this single ticket to life.

You other poets,
why carry on?
Unless to blind me
with your truth!

In Spain and Portugal

Postcard from Majorca

Nightingales hide
in valley thickets
on my holiday island,
where, when next
I am a nightingale
I too will sing
until evenings end
brings soft night
and flitting bats.

In the morning
I run down lanes
in human form
to hear nightingale song
where streams gurgle and play
under a footbridge
and snatches of molten notes
break and flood
from shady undergrowths.

Watch me kneel to place
the crown of my head
in these waters,
so cooling the brain
I run dripping
home again,
to reflect,
and breakfast on
honey, bread and tea.

Later, between hot hills
where the same waters spill
I sunbathe naked on a rock.
Lost in mid stream
I dream of mad
nightingale futures
finding solace in
small waterborne pebbles
to take home.

I have the pebbles now
and the waters somehow
still tumble them in my hand.
Nightingales sing
in quiet places yet,
no futures
are fast set,
and poets
still go running by.

Climbing in the Serra del Cavell Bernat

There is no track for me
in the Serra del Cavell Bernat.
Pushing straight up
from the roadside through
yellow thorn broom
onto limestone boulders
steep pitched and litter strewn,
I am breathless and hot,
carrying anxieties, regrets and triumphs
up to a smashed concrete plinth
that once advertised beer
to drivers on the road
some way below.

Looking on up, only blue sky and rock
of a broken ridge ascending.
Under my feet, the
eroded grey crag of a limestone reef
gives good grip for
my old running trainers
and feet, forty six years old,
confident of them yet
to carry me through
where others might fall,
though in another place one day
on a personal rock face
surely I must fail too.

Going further, someone lies resting
there on the rocks above me.
Hola I cry and
buenos dias to employ
my available Spanish,
knowing he will be surprised
to meet a fellow climber
where there is no path, just pain,
with a view of such distances
where no one ever came
before to discover
in himself, another place
where his loves might lie.

Wishing him well, I go on and up
trying every opportune step for advantage.
A hostile billy goat stares
and holds his ground on a high point
where both of us need to go,
he annoyed at my presence
in his solitary mountain fastness,
where surefootedness is life and
as he knows, nothing is to be gained
except the scent of rock rose
on hot mountain breezes.
He moves carefully away to
leave me with my own thorny ruminations.

man and goat left far below
I go on over false summits.
Anxieties, regrets and smashed plinths
are scattered in my way with
slippery dwarf palm leaves
and thorns that would trip
and tip me sideways,
to die slowly in a crevice
caught by broken foot or leg
with all dreams lost and shattered
on a waterless hillside,
unable to find myself in time
before the crows and buzzards do.

But say not yet die, for unexpectedly
I am on a pristine mountaintop.
Like life itself, greater peaks
stretch away to the distance,
faded in heat haze and set
by an aquamarine and cool
Mediterranean Ocean.
Beauty like love can
conquer all I think, or lead
to heartbreak on a hillside,
so I must turn and go down,
once again safe and sound,
hoping a mid life crisis will save me.

Days later I met a sun-struck fellow
on the high road from Formentor.
He had thrown signal rocks
down onto the roadway.
Naked but for shorts and
with bare feet, cut and bloody
he had been out two days he said
after losing his group,
he now needed water
and an emergency phone call.
Thought was, there by the grace go I,
so near have I come to disaster,
in my need to live sometimes faster.

Calypso

A hidden beach is always the best,
with sunshine and waves crashing,
and hippy shelters and nakedness allowed.

Here in the commune of the bamboo grove
Calypso and her friend have their place,
a rug under a collapsing fig tree.

Always a seagull floats left to right
as from the trodden sand,
a nude swimmer goes in for cooling.

Calypso, perfect brown in the shade of the brake,
washes her single garment
in the outpourings of a waterfall.

It dries itself on a wand,
while she lies given up
to the sun.

This is a place for secrets,
and promises,
as she turns to please her other side.

My Way

A Mediterranean night
gleams on the sea from my balcony
as wind ruffles and turns the pages
of Chapman's Homer,
my only companion to wine,

who tells me in whose fields,
far from their love'd own,
for Helen's sake and
forty ships to Trojan wars the
seas with him did pass.

I am absorbed, intoxicated,
as down the street a karaoke sings
I did it my –
way
on the warm night wind.

As if in the Alhambra

As if in a court of lions
rain falls constantly
and batters jasmine flowers
into temporary submission.

From this veranda
air is filled with water
and fountains drown
in the outpourings of their sister rain.

Sparrows scold in trees
and will not come down
for bread we set
in our lack of proper occupations,

as if we wait
in a hall of ambassadors,
to attend on beauty
from a long journey.

Rain stops
and a lid of grey
becomes a lid of blue
on our garden.

Always, exile from pleasure
is to raise our eyes to the mountains
and know well
the distant snows that live there.

Always, anticipation of pleasure
is to place our hands
in the fountain
and feel the rushing congress of water.

Always, fulfilment of pleasure
is not spoken of as we are gathered up
and pressed generously to heaven
desiring so much to stay there.

In the Alhambra

Haunted by an absence of things,
without Zoraya, the morning star,
a palace is just an empty cup.

No scent of jasmine or perfume
and only perfect marble underfoot
with the sun an orange ball of fire.

Sudden vistas are a distant silence
with only the chirruping of birds in eaves
and a breeze from off the mountain.

Poetry follows the beat of a camel-skin drum.
but no music plays, only the art of walls
and the sounding of a quiet fountain.

There is no rustling of silk,
no secret assignations made,
to the scrape of metal, or a command.

The wine is an empty cup
without Zoraya and her Sultan,
and their footsteps through the halls.

Alhama de Granada

Now with reading glasses
and the map of Sierra Tejeda,
we find Alhama again
in my solitary search for the Moor,
on the back roads of Granada.

See the discovered route that climbed
the mountain pass in driving rain,
car wipers slapping a beat
on the mule tracks from the coast,
to the Alhambra's timeless court.

Parking in the square
the sun came out weak yellow
on the walls of Abd Abdullah's fort,
Alhama de Granada,
the last he gave up before exile.

There still splashes the fount of the mosque,
near the house of the Inquisition,
shuttered up, while below in a bottomless gorge
an echoing cliff shuts the river in
between banks of white almond blossom.

I stuff my pockets
with the season's fallen nuts, and feast
on a warm orange in the shade,
where in this rush hour,
there is only a bleating of goats.

No grey city of the northern plain this!
Alhama is a forgotten dusty jewel
that I alone found through
close map reading
and poetic imagination.

But how to explain my
thirsting love of the place?
And the sudden burning need
to live there a summer or two
with a Scheherazade, to cook my meals.

A romance of Aljezur

The poet

It is dusk on the hill of Aljezur.
Tell me, do Moors still hold this castle?

No one answers,
for only poetry has a voice.

Come brave stones be reckless,
tell your story again.

Of fortune

The pine makes shade for cooling breezes
in the hot part of the day when nothing else stirs.

And fortune leads a man to watersides and
their grassy sward to hear the sound of sheep bells.

Green is the spring vestment that our lovely Alentejo
wears with plum blossom in her hair.

And summer colours dress her, as a mature woman
goes to the music of a dance.

Should a man admire loveliness as a virtue or
will his time be wasted in the souk with no business done?

My eyes are full of tears but my heart full of joy
at the memory of Beja and Mertola.

Beja, Mertola and the Alentjo are a wheat field where
the grain has been gathered too soon.

See the golden husks spilled to lie
in the great heat of our days.

Even the river Guadiana cannot wash
silver dust from the olive trees on the hills.

The olives and wheat fields of gleaming Beja and Mertola
float like a mirage and disappear.

Remember that Abd ar-Rahman was a falcon
whose tower looked out across the hills and the plain.

Now the highest in form and beauty
have fallen to be judged amongst the least.

And faith and passion no longer have a place
with the great merchant of the world.

It is as if the wild ass loose on the steppe
has been barred from its desert pasture and sweet flowers.

For ten summers I have celebrated
the memory of Beja and Mertola and their fallen excellence.

For ten winters I have stood to arms on the walls
of Aljezur and Silves looking to the north and the west.

But the cork oak and cistus forest is run through
and shaken by armed hosts everywhere.

While our resolve and our firebreaks have not stopped
the harsh winds that blow in our faces from every direction.

Can the small arrogance of a fool compare with the great
    arrogance
of one who opposes all through righteousness?

Separated from heaven, does a shooting star
know where it will fall?

Against fortune, the Captain of the castle
cannot turn his sturdy she-camel to the south.

For the Captain of the castle was wrought in the furnace of
    the desert
and the desert is an iron-masters workshop.

I wait to see if fortune will reproach me,
or if she will release me and place her hand in mine.

On love

At Silves there is a lamp that lights
every place of my heart, a singing girl.

She is small, slim waisted, strong of purpose with the body of
 a gazelle
and in her eyes the warming of the desert.

Her voice is a chiming of sheep's bells
in the mountains, rare with spice.

Her presence is perfume for a soldier
who rides to horse all day.

Her lips are plum blossom
in early spring.

In the dance her feet stamp like the oryx
scatter sand upon the dune.

In the dance her movements are the
beating of the camel-skin drum.

When she moves her breasts
are the voice of symbols shaken.

Her hips improve the rhythm of the tanbura
when the notes shiver to an ending.

So is the lamp she holds at night just myself
burning with oil from an endless reservoir?

Is the water jar bound with string she carries
from the well just the prison for my ambition?

Is the comb she weaves in her hair just my own sword
piercing my body with a carelessness that is hers?

Plentiful are the virtues of singing girls
when the entertainments are so generously bestowed.

Amongst such magnificence a purse of silver dirhams
would purchase but half a song.

Therefore I purchase Silves
with the full weight of my yet earth-bound soul.

My reward for the expense is one look
and shaken disdain from a small tambourine.

It follows that the deep arrogance of my heart would only be
    satisfied
by the pleasures of her complete surrender in love.

Equally I would surrender my castle and Aljezur
only to her, favoured Silves.

Know that the intricate pattern
of our exchange cannot be described in words.

Then behold nights when the separate tents of our
	wanderings
have been pitched together and I entered hers.

In her abode I accepted her embrace
and she pressed me to accept it.

In her abode I embraced her
and I pressed her to accept me.

There has never been and never will be another passion
to heat a man until the risen morning of the sun.

And we delayed the rising of the sun, in our unhurriedness
and immediate need to taste the fruits of the world.

Fruit that is hers that she shares with an endless generosity
but strictly rationed.

The arrival of new day is like the breaking of potsherds
so that no vessel is left to carry water.

Amongst the potsherds I wait, I starve, the day is only thirst
and the night full of longings.

On war

Keeping an even measure of days
The caravans come in from the waste.

While war is a sandstorm that pushes our walls
And forces the chinks in our gate.

Our castle has two towers, like brothers
shouldering their stones for faith.

The towers are an arrow's flight to the bridge,
Where arrows fly like a swift at the cry.

Suddenly our black dogs leap at their chains
to proclaim their rightful inheritance,

as the morning light comes up shrouded,
pinned between mountain and cloud.

See our spears grown cold from the still night air,
piled in a single sheaf at the gate.

But my sword wears a hard edge and beads of moisture,
in being taken early from the scabbard.

And know that this day is for armour and that straps chafe
in their eagerness for the strike.

I will be first to the metal and those who follow me
will find me in the very thickest of the fighting.

In war, arrogance is a virtue, when fortune decides that
mountains must be lifted from the plain and rivers made to
flow backwards.

Like rain from the north and west their armies come, their
host,
with banners lifting like crows and lightening flickering in
their ranks

With a light that is not light,
connecting heaven and earth and burning it.

The sun hides her face
though we look for it.

Horses toss their heads to stamp from their stalls,
eyes resisting fear.

Our spears raised are few
and many points are shivered, waiting for the on come.

But my curved sword is of the fire and the furnace
and it takes its edge from the light of the sun.

It is a sword from the great desert of the south
where lives are easily taken.

Unsheathed, it is for Aljezur and Silves
and it flashes like a mirror held high.

The sword advances at the trot
and our soldiers press forward to admire it.

At once my horse is spurred for the bridge
and her hooves thunder on the boards and are over it.

Hear the shout arise from the great host
at the approaching sword,

Riding for the heart's blood
and the rain.

The poet

Sun and water make the valley of Aljezur fertile
and deep soil brings rich harvests.

Beja, Mertola, Silves and Aljezur continue
in the quiet poetry of their lives.

The singing girl and the flashing sword are immortal,
their bodies slaves of history as well as those of lovers.

I release them in the closing of the page.

A mirror for Portugal

Morning

Where has night gone?
Daylight has the room
like white horses
leave no hiding place for sleep,
and morning stirs
to distant voices
and a moped, climbing
a new bright hill.

Remember, if we can,
life before new worlds,
and how we flew
over cumulous clouds
to be laid like an egg
on the tarmac,
hatching a phoenix
from stratospheres of blue.

Through closed shutters,
rainbows
float with dust,
dazzling a sleeper awakened,
lifting him in the air
with birds who twitter,
for night is gone
and his dreams undone.

If the shutters opened,
they would tell
of how days begin,
ending dreams
of horse drawn diligences,
and sailing boats rising
on tides to anchor
under Moorish castle walls.

A thousand swifts
conspired to bring me here,
hear them chase
in close formation,
as I cross the room bare foot
to wrest the shutters open
and confound them, lined up
on my single telephone wire.

Lifting the catch
light spills everywhere,
and the world breathes vapour
rising from rooftops below,
last dew warmed
in early steaming sun,
calling midge flies
to come and rise for breakfast.

Now wash the sleep from our eyes,
harvest last night's stubble
and attend to necessary ships,
mules and diligences.
The distant moped
has carried the day,
and it clatters out of town
with a vengeance.

At the roadside

Pulling over to park up,
the stopped engine
is killed by silence
descended from the hills,
filling the valley
and open windows,
as cooling metal
ticks away the stillness.

Reflected in the mirror,
a dirt road
bends to hide
between folding cistus hills,
trying to be a river gone dry,
unsure how to empty itself
in the confusion of light and colour,
meadows and cork oak.

There is no point in locking up.
Take the path with its perfumed air
and debris of seasons,
that makes numerous hidey-holes
for lizards bright as buttons,
who never saw a person before
in a million years
of tourism.

Across a meadow
belonging to the sun,
hear the goddess
of small falling waters,
and her fair acolytes
corn marigold and statice, singing,
fallen in love
with trains of winnowing grasses.
What dim remembered farm
is this, of marigolds,
butterflies and cork oak?
Tread the tinders softly,
for every bush
has birds calling
as if we were in England,
go back! go back! go back!

Three-second arias burst
from closet streams,
short songs of lost love
from behind the rampant fig,
piercing the broken
windows and shutters
of a house that waited
for rain too long, and its healing.

Yes! As if we were in England
we sweat like a ploughman
under an agricultural hat,
furrows crumbling to dust,
with the marauding
and hooligan birds
shouting where ya go-in?
go back! go back! go back!

In the end, the valley had
only fourteen beehives
standing in a row,
to miles of shimmering
cistus covered hills
flowering creamy white,
and their lazy buzzing
warning us to go.

Noon in the Alentejo

Always long and always empty,
Alentejo roads flicker
tree lined at speed,
melted in heat,
through brilliant parklands
of wheat and holly oak,
whose opening parasols
make picnic shades of hillsides.

It's always forty kilometres
to the next small café,
where old senhors
sit all day in the bus stop,
hand on stick, cap on head,
talking and counting
every passing
car and courtesy.

There the tan brown hound
sleeps in the road
or whatever shade he can find
from the burning cobbles,
rising with a mournful gaze
of sacrifice, for cars
that must always be going,
somewhere.

This once famous town
climbs the hill yet
proclaiming loyalty
to past wars and sometimes victory,
as the church bell clangs, din-din
at the empty approaching roads,
pointing like compass arrows
at the heart.

On the still square at noon,
a street arch frames
oil portraits of the town,
gathering her skirts
at the plains we crossed,
with only silver wheat,
pale olives and oaks drawn
to the faint hills beyond.

In that vertiginous heat,
we retreat to the alcazar,
the ruined Arab fortress
holding high promontory
over bends in the river,
whose ribbon shoals
filled last year, they say,
and where ghosts of children still play.

Forty kilometres on,
in the snack bar Descana Pernas,
English is surprisingly spoken
there's no privacy
in a nuclear sub you don't
even get your own bed,
and we sip our café con leite,
agradecido, so thankful.

Returning to the world,
a route national
cuts through the bones of the land,
directed to Sines, Lisboa
and Espana, every
vehiculo longo articulating
commerce through the thin
arteries of the nation.
Alentejo is a distant mirage.

Siesta

Siesta is an outrageous luxury,
that probes the far bounds of consciousness,
where mopeds arrive and depart
in shady garage assignations,
or wait put putting outside the
shuttered quietness of rooms,
whose walls and ceilings recede
like magnolia ghosts of night,
leaving still pools of air
to reflect the last ripples,
of imagination.

In long moments we
listen before sleep
to the dun sound of cow bells
dingling in valleys,
cows who know that
nothing happens in the
middle of the day,
when the grazing hours
stretch out without limit
and the pointless two legged people
cease their meandering about.

Then we must
stand or sleep
to the ding dang
of a church bell,
on the hour every hour,
from a distant tower
of ecclesiastical timekeeping,
religion the last thing we hear
before sleep overtakes us,
perhaps even forever,
in her cool bosomed pillows.

Wakened, already are we?
A butterfly
flies in at the door,
circles once and
goes out again.
Was that glimpse
an inhabitant,
or our imagination freed
to conjure spirits
of something, or someone
we know?

The lemon tree

Picking a lemon from her tree
my neighbour Visinia
explains the uses of the gift
in flowering Portuguese,
that my few learned words
understand but little.

But travel is a mirror
held up to ourselves
and in the mirror
the lemon given
is a fruit as bright
as the sun.

Obrigado Visinia,
full grateful
for the treasure,
we know how when
times come to part,
all is not gone and lost forever.

The coming of night

Birdsong rings long past sunset
until night brings a
quick breeze and
skies die a small cold death
over bare hills,
where we went.

We walk not far down the lane
to test the stillness of things
and remember, remember nothing.

A bat comes and goes
on a whisper of air,
while a dog barks
just because he must,
a mile or more away,
where a moped stuttered
when the day was long,
and life had just begun,
hadn't it?

The dim light on the lane
is not enough
to stop chill rising
in the valley below
and the frog chorus starting
reep reep, reep reep,
all the world's asleep,
except for you, who who,
says the soft owl kind,
waking from her sleep
in the tall fir bough,
to see mice and men,
moving in the lane again.

Frogs get intimate
and ratchet up the noise with
the hollow reed cicadas
chirruping a distant racket,
as we turn, wonderfully,
to a nightingale,
who can't keep quiet at night
and sings from his dream
as if the morning light he's seen,
his sudden loving torment
splits the stony brake
when all the world's in bed
except, for no one.

Indoors now through
inky windows
the moon rises
pale, yellow and silent,
faster than you'd think
over the old town,
where a lone dog
barks one last time
to remind us
of midnight,
bedtime,
and bright
tomorrows.